Beverley MacDonald
CARTOONS BY Andrew Weldon

IT'S TRUE!

Crime
DOESn'T
PAY

ALLEN&UNWIN

First published in 2004

Allen & Unwin
83 Alexander Street
Crows Nest NSW 2065
Australia
Phone: (61 2) 8425 0100
Fax: (61 2) 9906 2218
Email: info@allenandunwin.com
Web: www.allenandunwin.com

National Library of Australia
Cataloguing-in-Publication entry:

MacDonald, Beverley.
It's true! Crime doesn't pay.
Bibliography.
Includes index.
ISBN 1 74114 275 X.
1. Criminal investigation – History – Juvenile literature. 2. Criminology
– History – Juvenile literature. I. Weldon, Andrew, 1971– . II. Title.
364

Series, cover and text design by Ruth Grüner
Cover photograph: Photodisc Collection/Getty Images
Set in 12.5pt Minion by Ruth Grüner
Printed by McPherson's Printing Group

1 3 5 7 9 10 8 6 4 2

**Teaching notes for the It's True! series are available
on the website: www.itstrue.com.au**

IT'S TRUE!

Crime
DOESn'T
PAY

Other  IT'S TRUE! titles

There Are Bugs in Your Bed
Heather Catchpole and Vanessa Woods
PICTURES BY Craig Smith

Pigs Do Fly
Terry Denton
PICTURES BY Terry Denton

Your Hair Grows 15 Kilometres a Year
Diana Lawrenson
PICTURES BY Leigh Hobbs

Frogs Are Cannibals
Michael Tyler
PICTURES BY Mic Looby

The Romans Were the Real Gangsters
John and Joshua Wright
PICTURES BY Joshua Wright

CONTENTS

WHY CRIME?

Like many writers, I'm interested in just about everything. I like to know how things work and how people think. I want to know why things happened, how they happened and what happened next.

In some ways it's what detectives do – piecing together a story from the clues. I believe what criminals do is wrong, but understanding how criminals think and how police detectives catch them is fascinating all the same. And judging by all the popular TV shows about crime-fighters and forensic scientists, I'm not the only one.

I hope you enjoy these stories.

Beverley Ma

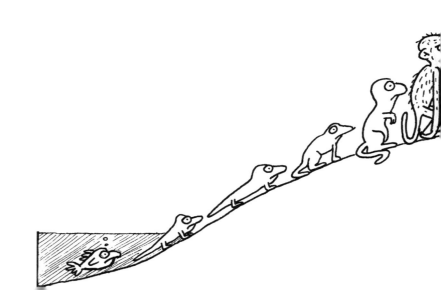

1

HISTORY'S FIRST THIEF?

GIVE MONEY,
HOMO SAPIENS
SCUM!

Crime has always been with us. Perhaps it began something like this . . .

A long long time ago, a Stone Age man looked at his friend's fine new stone axe and thought, 'I'd like that.' He may have offered his friend a string of beads in exchange for the axe, and his friend refused. Maybe he had nothing to offer. But he wanted that axe.

1

He needed that axe. He couldn't live without that axe. What should he do? He came up with a new idea. He decided the easiest way to get what he wanted was to steal it. And so he did. He became history's very first thief.

We know there was crime in ancient times because people made up laws about what was wrong, and how wrongdoers should be punished. If there hadn't been any crime they wouldn't have needed to.

Nearly 4000 years ago in Babylon, the first *written* laws were carved into a huge column of rock for everybody to see. King Hammurabi's code of laws was tough.

If a man puts out the eye of another man,
    his eye shall be put out.
If he breaks another man's bone,
    his bone shall be broken.

Thieves had their hands cut off!

There was a long list of crimes where the punishment was death. They included assisting

THE UNDETERRED THIEF

runaway slaves, breaking into houses, stealing children, bearing false witness (telling lies to a judge), and stealing from a temple.

But what were the chances of getting caught? How do you catch a thief? How do you tell who is lying and who is telling the truth? Who is guilty and who is innocent?

2

GUILTY OR INNOCENT?

The Old Testament of the Bible suggested that if a husband thought his wife might be having an affair with another man, he should sweep up all the dirt from the floor of the temple, mix it with water and make his wife drink it. If she got sick, she was guilty, and if she didn't, she was probably innocent.

These trials were called 'ordeals'. People believed that God (or supernatural powers) would protect innocent people and punish the guilty.

A dispute between two men could be decided in an *ordeal by combat*. The men would fight to decide who was right and who was wrong. God would ensure that the innocent man won and the guilty person lost. Of course, big strong men were usually right and skinny little guys were usually found guilty.

An *ordeal by hot metal* wasn't any more reliable. In medieval England an accused man was forced to hold a red-hot iron bar in his bare hands and walk for nine paces. If his hands were burned, he was pronounced guilty and hanged.

Worse still was an *ordeal by water*. It was a popular way of identifying witches in the Middle Ages. If a woman was suspected of being a witch she would be tied up in a sack and thrown into a pond.

If she drowned, she was innocent (witches floated), and if she didn't drown she was obviously a witch and was burned alive at the stake! It was a 'no-win' situation for the woman – either way she ended up dead.

TRIAL BY DONKEY

In India it was a case of *trial by donkey*. First, a donkey was tied up in a dark room with no windows and only a single door. Then the village headman summoned all the people who might have committed the crime. He explained that the donkey had magical powers.

'Those who are innocent need have no fear,' the headman said. 'But the donkey will know who is guilty. It will bray when that man pulls its tail.'

I WANT YOU TO GO INTO THAT DARK ROOM WITH THAT DONKEY.

He then instructed each man to enter the room and pull the donkey's tail.

The trial began.

One by one the men entered the room, and as they left, the headman inspected their hands. The villagers waited expectantly, but the donkey remained silent. Finally, the last man emerged from the room. The villagers looked at each other. Was no one guilty?

Then the headman spoke.

'That man is guilty!' He pointed to one of the men.

The accused man hung his head and confessed his guilt. The rest of the villagers were amazed. How had the donkey known?

What really happened? While no one was looking the headman covered the donkey's tail in black soot. All the innocent men confidently pulled the donkey's tail and got soot on their hands. One man, the guilty one, didn't touch the donkey's tail because he believed it would know he was guilty. He was the only person to come out with clean hands.

3

BEFORE THERE WERE POLICE

CATCHING CROOKS

Throughout history people could be convicted (found guilty) and punished if . . .

They were *caught* doing the crime.

They were *seen* doing the crime.

They *confessed* to doing the crime.

If a thief was caught stealing from a shop, there was no question that he was guilty. The shopkeeper could deal out his own punishment and give the thief a beating. If the crime was really serious, the thief would be brought before the local headman (or prince, or priest) to decide the punishment.

If the thief got away, but was seen stealing from the shop, witnesses were called to testify to what they saw. Whether the thief was found guilty depended on who the witnesses were. Everybody believed that important people always told the truth and ordinary people told the truth sometimes. (Women were supposed to be too unreliable to ever tell the truth, and they weren't allowed to testify. This is still the case in some countries today.)

Of course, if the criminal confessed to his crime he could also be convicted and punished. A suspected criminal could be tortured to gain a confession.

Whether a person was tortured depended on who they were. About 2000 years ago in Ancient Rome it was against the law to torture citizens. Anybody else *could* be tortured, and slaves *had* to be tortured (because people believed slaves were natural liars and wouldn't tell the truth otherwise). Torture as a way of extracting confessions remained popular over many centuries. The Catholic Church tortured witches and heretics (people who didn't agree with the Church). Kings and queens tortured their enemies.

In fact, nothing much changed for about the next seventeen centuries.

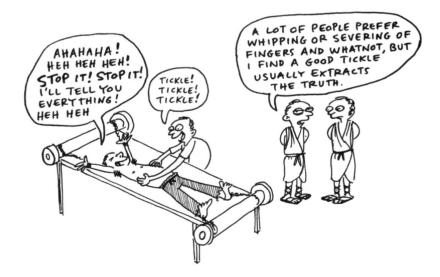

DRUNKS AND HIGHWAYMEN

During the eighteenth century (the 1700s), the population of London grew to over half a million people. It was one of the biggest cities in the world. The roads were muddy and dark and unlit at night. Most people lived in small, damp, nasty little houses. Thirty people could live in one room. There was high unemployment and people were sent to jail for owing money or being in debt. Children were sent out to work as soon as they turned six. Conditions were pretty bad, but they were about to get a lot worse.

A new drink came on the market: gin. It was cheap and easy to make. For the first time, even poor people could afford to get drunk, and a lot of them did. There was a popular saying, 'Drunk for a penny, dead drunk for two pennies'. Even babies were given gin to make them stop crying and go to sleep!

These were desperate times. It was no wonder there was a crime wave. Pickpockets and thieves roamed the alleys, stealing purses and handkerchiefs. People were robbed at knifepoint for enough money to buy something to eat, or a place to sleep, or even another drink.

It was no better outside London. Highwaymen held up coaches at gunpoint, demanding money and jewellery from terrified travellers.

Something had to be done.

HANGING AND TRANSPORTATION

The government was desperate. They hoped harsher penalties might stop the crime wave. They increased the number of crimes punishable by hanging to 350. People were hanged for sheep-stealing, forgery,

house-breaking, highway robbery, burning down
a house, poaching a rabbit, or even cutting down
an ornamental bush.

It didn't work. The crime wave continued to rise.
The government finally realised they couldn't hang
everyone. So someone came up with a new idea – to
send convicted criminals overseas where they would
be someone else's problem.

Convicts were transported to the new British
colonies in America, where they were put to work

clearing land and building roads. But in 1775 the Americans fought a war against England and won their independence. America refused to take any more convicts. The jails in England began to fill up again. For a while the government used broken-down ships as jails, but there weren't enough ships to house all the convicts.

Luckily, Captain Cook had discovered a new continent a few years earlier, and in 1788 eleven ships landed in Sydney Harbour with their cargo of convicts. They were destined to found the new 'thief-colony' of Australia. But, as with hanging, the government couldn't transport everyone, and in 1857 transportation came to an end.

The English government had to find another way to stop the crime wave. They tried offering a large reward to anyone who captured a highwayman. There was still no such thing as a police force, but some people became professional 'thief-takers'. Often they were criminals who captured their fellow criminals for the reward money.

THE AMAZING LIFE OF
JONATHAN WILD

Jonathan Wild was a young man who'd already spent four years of his life in prison for debt. While he was in jail he learned a lot about crime and criminals.

When he was released, he decided to set himself up as a thief-taker. He declared that for a small reward he would find the stolen goods and return them to their owners.

What he really did was contact the thief and offer him some of the reward money in return for the goods. The people who got their stolen goods back were happy and he was well paid for his efforts.

If a thief refused to agree to Wild's scheme, he would arrest them and hand them over to the authorities. No matter what happened, Wild still received the reward. It was an almost fool-proof system.

Wild hired assistants, and for more than ten years he controlled much of the crime in London. He arrested so many criminals, he became rich and famous.

He declared himself 'Thief-Taker General of

Great Britain and Ireland'. The government even asked him for advice on how to curb highway robberies.

'Increase the reward money!' Wild suggested.

The government took his advice and more than doubled the reward. Wild became ever richer and more famous. He was responsible for sending hundreds of convicts to be hanged at the gallows. But it didn't last. The public grew suspicious of Jonathan Wild – instead of believing he was a crime-fighting hero they thought he was just another crook.

Eventually he was arrested for buying stolen goods from a thief. He was found guilty and hanged in front of a large jeering crowd.

THE BOW STREET RUNNERS

Jonathan Wild was not forgotten. A playwright named Henry Fielding wrote a best-selling novel about Wild's life. Fielding said that if the government gave him some money he would deal with London's rising crime rate. The government took him up on his offer and gave him a grant.

Henry Fielding rented a building in Bow Street and hired men who knew all the local criminals by sight. His system was simple. Anyone who was robbed went straight to Bow Street and described the thief, and Fielding's men would immediately take off running after the suspect.

Believe it or not, the Bow Street Runners usually caught their man still with the loot in his pocket. In those days criminals weren't used to being pursued, and they often went home or down the pub afterwards.

Henry Fielding's plan worked, and the crime rate dropped dramatically. Later, the government set up road patrols of heavily armed horsemen and the number of highway robberies dropped sharply as well.

Of course, criminals quickly worked out how to take the new Bow Street Runners into their plans. They made sure they had fast getaway horses. They covered their faces so they wouldn't be recognised. They got rid of the loot as quickly as possible. The crime rate began to rise again.

Finally, in 1829, the government set up a new crime-fighting force. The Metropolitan Police were given headquarters at New Scotland Yard in London. This was the first modern police force. At first the public weren't very impressed with men in uniforms patrolling the streets. On several occasions people stood by and watched while policemen were attacked and murdered. It took another twenty years before the public finally changed their mind.

SET A THIEF TO CATCH A THIEF

In Paris in the early 1800s, a very handsome young man named Eugène-François Vidocq decided he was sick of being a criminal. He'd been in trouble all his life because of his love of gambling and women. He owed money to lots of people. To get out of debt he'd tried his hand at smuggling, but he was caught and sent to prison. He didn't like jail and he escaped and was recaptured. Now he was in real trouble.

He was set to spend the rest of his life in jail.

Vidocq tried to make a deal. He offered to inform on his fellow criminals if the authorities would not increase his jail sentence. Instead, they offered to release him if he became a police spy. Vidocq wasn't keen on the idea. He knew how criminals dealt with informers and spies. He was likely to be killed. The police threatened to lay new charges against him which would mean he'd never get out of jail. In the end, Vidocq had no choice. He agreed.

The police arranged for Vidocq to stage a 'daring escape' from jail, and by the time he secretly returned to Paris he was famous. All the other criminals trusted

him and took him into their confidence. For many years Vidocq was an extremely crafty and successful police spy. He became a master of disguise, and personally arrested many criminals, and his brave, daring exploits became the talk of Paris.

Once Vidocq found out that a very dangerous and violent criminal had left some belongings at a house. While the rest of the police force scoured the streets of Paris, Vidocq waited patiently hidden in the house for several days until the criminal finally returned to collect his possessions. After a desperate struggle, Vidocq captured the man single-handed.

Vidocq kept written records about all the criminals he knew, and he was so successful that the government made him the first head of its criminal investigation department.

But within a few years Vidocq was accused of corruption and forced to resign. He promptly set himself up as a private investigator and wrote his memoirs, which became a best-seller. Vidocq's story and crime-fighting techniques inspired a new generation of writers and police investigators.

4

WRITERS INVENT DETECTIVES

Another writer, Charles Dickens, knew from experience how tough life could be in nineteenth-century England. When he was only twelve years old, his father was sent to prison for debt. Charles had to leave school and go to work in a factory to support his family. For many years he was desperately poor and unhappy. He wrote stories to earn extra money, and was eventually so successful that he became a full-time writer.

Dickens wrote about his early experiences in one of his most famous novels, *Oliver Twist* – the story of a young pauper boy sent to live in a workhouse. Dickens described how the children in workhouses were treated. They were always hungry and cold. They were treated cruelly and often beaten. There was no escape. In the novel, when Oliver finally ran away from the workhouse he was forced to join a gang of young pickpockets in London and become a criminal. There was a happy ending to Oliver Twist's story, but it was not the same for most poor children in real life. People were shocked by Dickens' stories.

While Dickens was writing his stories, public executions were still taking place in London.

The government believed that watching criminals hang would discourage people from a life of crime. But it had absolutely no effect on the crime rate.

Public hangings were a popular source of entertainment. Vendors sold snacks and beer and gin, and sometimes more than 20 000 people turned up to watch. People would pay for seats with a good view of the scaffold. It was a bit like going to the footy. Occasionally things got out of hand and there were riots. People were crushed to death or trampled in the panic.

In 1849 Charles Dickens paid for good seats to watch a particularly interesting hanging. A husband and wife had been found guilty of murder, and were to be hanged together on the same scaffold. Dickens was so upset by what he saw that day that he began to write articles condemning public executions. He thought they were barbaric.

Dickens became interested in crime and crime-fighting. He read about Wild and Vidocq. He decided the new police were a good idea, and wrote articles that helped changed the public's attitude towards them.

Charles Dickens was even responsible for inventing 'detective police'. The very first detective was not a real person, but a character in one of his books – Inspector Bucket in his novel *Bleak House*.

POLICE H.Q.

GENTLEMEN! I'VE FOUND JUST THE MAN TO SOLVE LONDON'S CRIME PROBLEM! — INSPECTOR BUCKET!

UNFORTUNATELY HE'S FICTIONAL, BUT WE'RE WORKING ON THAT PROBLEM...

DETECTIVE STORIES

Another writer was responsible for inventing the detective story.

Edgar Allan Poe lived a short and miserable life. He was an orphan whose foster-father hated him. He was thrown out of school and university and military college, and sacked from several jobs. He took up drinking and became an alcoholic. He wrote sensational and shocking stories to make a living. He wrote stories about people who were accidentally buried alive, and stories about murderers and people tortured by the Spanish Inquisition.

Poe created an eccentric investigator who solved crimes by carefully examining the clues and reconstructing the crime according to the evidence. Poe's character Auguste Dupin first appeared in his novel *The Murders in the Rue Morgue*. It is the most famous early detective novel, yet the word 'detective' does not appear in it once.

Another writer, Arthur Conan Doyle, created the most famous literary detective.

Conan Doyle was a rather unsuccessful doctor who started writing sensational stories to make some extra money. He knew about the exploits of Wild and Vidocq, and he'd read the stories of Charles Dickens and Edgar Allan Poe.

Doyle created his famous character, Sherlock Holmes – a brilliant and extremely eccentric private detective who solved unsolvable crimes by using deductive reasoning and logic.

When a young woman arrived unannounced at Sherlock Holmes' house, he explained that he already knew a lot about her – that she'd arrived by carriage after a journey from the countryside and had come to ask for his help. She was astounded and asked him how he knew.

Holmes explained his reasoning. He'd noticed a fine spray of mud on one of her gloves, yet her shoes were clean. There was no mud in the city streets, so she must have come from outside the city. Her shoes weren't muddy, so she didn't walk. And the pattern of the mud on her glove was consistent with that sprayed up from a carriage's wheels. She must have rested her gloved hand on the carriage's window. And why else would she arrive unannounced after a long journey if not to ask him for help? She agreed he was absolutely right.

Sherlock Holmes declared:

'When you have eliminated all which is impossible, then whatever remains, however improbable, must be the truth.'

SHERLOCK HOLME BOY

ELEMENTARY M.C. WATSON.

26

BOOK SOLVES MURDER MYSTERY

In 1881 the German police were called to a crime scene. A man named Fritz Conrad had discovered the bodies of his wife and five young children inside a locked room. The police were baffled by what they discovered.

The first thing the inspector in charge of the case did was to examine the room carefully. Both the door and the window were bolted from inside. There was no way into the room from outside. It looked as though the woman had killed her children and then herself. But the inspector wasn't satisfied.

The inspector spoke to the husband, who insisted he was innocent. The door was bolted from inside, so how could he possibly be involved? Without further evidence the inspector had to agree that the man was probably telling the truth. It sounded like the only reasonable explanation.

But the inspector still felt something wasn't quite right.

He examined the room again, and was just about to leave when he picked up a book from the shelf.

The book was *Nena Sahib* by John Ratcliffe. It fell open
at a spot that had obviously been read many times.
The inspector was astounded. The book described how
a man murdered someone in a room and made it look
like a suicide.

Quickly the inspector crossed the room and
re-examined the door. Underneath the bolt he
discovered a tiny hole drilled in the wood. On the outer
side of the door was a smear of brown wax. When he
scraped away the wax with his fingernail he could see
the other end of the hole.

'Arrest that man for murder!' He pointed to the dead woman's husband.

Fritz Conrad was tried in court, found guilty and executed.

How did Fritz Conrad bolt the door from outside? He used the method described in the novel. First he drilled a tiny hole through the door. Then he inserted a horsehair through the hole and tied one end to the bolt. (Horsehair is very strong.) He locked the door from outside by pulling on the horsehair until the bolt closed. Afterwards he covered the hole on the outside of the door with sealing wax. If only Fritz Conrad had remembered to throw away the book, he might have got away with murder!

5

IDENTITY PARADE

The creation of a police force marked the beginning of a new attitude towards crime. Instead of inventing stronger locks and bigger guns to deter criminals, people began to use their intelligence. The next important step in modern policing took place in France – the introduction of scientific method to crime-fighting.

WHO IS IT?

Identifying people has been a problem for a long time.

In 1725 a human head was found lying on the banks of the Thames River at Westminster in England. Nobody knew whose it was. The local magistrate ordered that the head be mounted on a pole and displayed in the churchyard, in the hope that someone might recognise it.

Sure enough, it didn't take long for a neighbour to identify the head as belonging to the missing husband of a local woman. She was Catherine Hayes, who had told everyone her husband had gone abroad.

MADAM, DO YOU RECOGNISE THIS STINKING, DISEMBODIED HEAD?

WELL, FROM THE SMELL I'D SAY IT'S MY YOUNGEST — HAROLD JUNIOR, BUT HE STILL HAS HIS ATTACHED.

Catherine Hayes was arrested and questioned. Finally she confessed that she'd talked her lover into murdering her husband. The lover was hanged for his part in the murder, and she was burned alive. At the time only women were burned at the stake, as it was considered a less severe punishment than hanging!

Of course, it wasn't always possible to identify a body by displaying it in public.

An even bigger problem was the identification of criminals. Crooks knew they probably wouldn't be recognised outside their neighbourhood. They started doing their crimes in other cities and towns. They gave false names when they were arrested. It was almost impossible to connect criminals with previous crimes and convictions. The same person could be wanted under several different names in the same city.

The first camera was invented in 1835, and police departments soon began photographing criminals for

FOR GOD'S SAKE MEN
—JUST HOLD HIS
FACIAL MUSCLES
STILL JUST ONE
MINUTE LONGER!

UNGK!

identification. But at the time photography was a very slow process, and unless the person sat completely still for fifteen minutes while the photograph was taken, it would be blurred and unrecognisable. Needless to say, criminals weren't very helpful about sitting still. An easier, quicker way of identifying people was needed.

THE BUMPS ON YOUR HEAD

In 1796 a Viennese doctor, Dr Franz Josef Gall, declared he had discovered a method of identifying a person's characters by the shape of their head. A bump at the back of the skull meant you had domestic tendencies (and should do all the cooking and cleaning), bumps just above your ears meant you were selfish, bumps at the front meant you were very smart, and so on.

The theory of *phrenology* became very popular over the next century. People believed that by taking careful measurements of people's skulls you could identify those with criminal tendencies.

In 1876 a French doctor published his study of 6000 criminals, and declared he could identify 'the criminal face'. Pickpockets were tall and dark with long hands. Highwaymen had thick hair. Arsonists had small heads. According to the doctor, even con men could be recognised by their wide jaws and strong cheekbones.

There was absolutely no scientific proof for either theory, but over the decades many criminals had their heads meticulously measured and re-measured and checked for bumps. Neither theory helped with the basic problem of identifying people.

PHRENOLOGY

THE BUMPS ON YOUR SON'S HEAD WOULD INDICATE THAT NOT ONLY DOES HE HAVE CRIMINAL TENDENCIES, BUT HE IS SPAWN OF SATAN, LORD OF DARKNESS.

BORED CLERK MEASURES PEOPLE

Alphonse Bertillon was an extremely bored clerk
stuck behind a desk in a Parisian police station.
He began to wonder if all these measurements could be
used for another purpose. Instead of revealing people
with criminal tendencies, maybe they could be used
to establish identity. Did everybody have a unique set
of measurements?

Bertillon convinced the head of the police
department to let him try out his idea. He spent three
months carefully measuring and cross-checking before
he finally found a match.

A criminal arrested under the name of Dupont
had the same measurements as a Monsieur Martin,
a known and convicted thief. When the police
questioned Dupont he admitted that yes, he was indeed
Martin the thief. The French police were impressed and
decided to adopt Bertillon's system.

FINGERPRINTS

Alas, Bertillon's success didn't last for long. A much better and simpler way of identifying people was discovered: fingerprints. It wasn't a totally new idea.

In ancient China 3000 years ago, legal documents were signed and sealed with fingerprints. The Japanese adopted the same system. But it wasn't until 1860 that an English civil servant working in India decided to use fingerprints to identify people. He suspected pensioners were turning up more than once to collect their pension money. As most of them were illiterate, it was no use asking them to sign their name when they collected the money. He came up with the idea of using their fingerprints. It worked. He could prove they had already collected their pension by matching their prints.

As happens with a lot of good ideas, someone else was working on it at the same time. After his house was burgled, a Scottish doctor working in Japan became convinced every single fingerprint was unique. Unfortunately it took many days, or even several weeks, to compare a single fingerprint against all the fingerprint files. It just wasn't practical to use fingerprints.

When an Englishman, Sir Francis Galton, invented a way to classify fingerprints, it finally meant the files could be quickly searched and cross-checked. He divided fingerprints into four basic patterns; arches, whorls, loops and composites.

The most common fingerprint pattern is the loop, which accounts for two-thirds of all human fingerprints. Slightly less than one-third of people have whorl ridge patterns, and one in twenty people have arches. Loops can slant to the right or the left, whorls can be plain, double, central-pocket and accidental; arches can be smooth or pointed; or a print may have composites of various groups.

The USA was one of the first and most enthusiastic supporters of fingerprinting, all because of one man.

In 1924 the legendary J. Edgar Hoover was appointed director of the FBI (Federal Bureau of Investigation). He turned the FBI into an efficient crime-fighting body and established not only a fingerprinting bureau, but also scientific crime-detection laboratories.

Over the next few years the FBI turned its attention to organised crime and arrested many major gangsters (including Al Capone). Within a few years there were over 800 000 prints on file, and in 1967 the system was computerised. Today the FBI's fingerprint files contain over 200 million prints and is the largest collection in the world.

Fingerprints can also be used to help solve crimes.

There are three kinds of prints left at a crime scene:

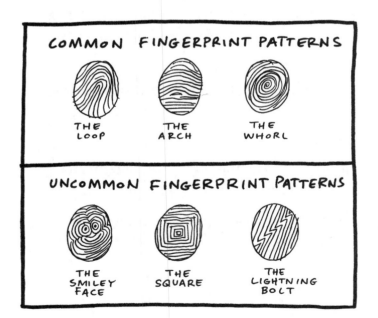 *visible* prints left by things such as paint, ink or blood;

plastic prints left on surfaces like soap or wax;

and *latent* prints which are made by sweat. (There are always tiny traces of body oils and perspiration on our skin, even if we can't feel them).

COMMON FINGERPRINT PATTERNS

THE LOOP

THE ARCH

THE WHORL

UNCOMMON FINGERPRINT PATTERNS

THE SMILEY FACE

THE SQUARE

THE LIGHTNING BOLT

Latent prints may not be visible until a crime investigator dusts the surface with a powder that sticks to the oily perspiration.

Different powders are used for different surfaces; black carbon powder for light-coloured surfaces, and white aluminium powder on dark surfaces. Fluorescent powders are used on brightly coloured and patterned surfaces, and are visible under ultra-violet light.

New techniques for revealing latent prints are still being developed. For difficult surfaces such as the inside of plastic bags, forensic scientists use the fumes from hot superglue. The active ingredient in superglue will stick to the faintest trace of fingerprints.

Latent prints must be photographed or lifted on 'stickytape' to make a permanent record.

THE SHARK ARM MURDER

On 25 April 1935, at Sydney's Coogee Beach aquarium, a large crowd of people watched as a recently captured tiger shark began to thrash around in the water. The shark was obviously in distress. The people watching were even more upset when the shark vomited up a human arm! People screamed and fainted.

Aquarium staff quickly removed the arm and sent it to the morgue for examination. It was a well-muscled arm with a distinctive tattoo, but no one knew who it belonged to. It didn't match the description of any missing person in the police files.

Who did the arm belong to? Where was the rest of the body? Had there been an accident at sea, or had something more sinister happened?

Even though the skin was very fragile, the scientists finally managed to piece together a recognisable fingerprint. They found that it belonged to James Smith, an ex-boxer who had been known to hang out with criminals. The police questioned his wife, who explained that about two weeks earlier her husband had said he was going fishing with a friend. She didn't know who the friend was, but her husband hadn't returned, and she hadn't seen him since.

The police immediately suspected that Smith's criminal friends were involved. But a vital witness was murdered before the police could make an arrest, and in the end the mystery was never solved. Nor was the rest of James Smith's body ever recovered. Even so, without the fingerprints Mrs Smith would never have known whether her husband was alive or dead.

THE SHARK ARM FUNERAL

'EVERY CONTACT LEAVES A TRACE'

The very first scientific crime laboratory was set up in France in 1910. A scientist named Edmund Locard was a big fan of the Sherlock Holmes detective stories. He admired the way Holmes used the smallest trace of evidence to work out what had happened at the scene of a crime. Locard thought the same scientific approach to collecting and analysing evidence could be used in real life. He developed his famous principle 'Every contact leaves a trace'. It became known as Locard's Principle of Exchange.

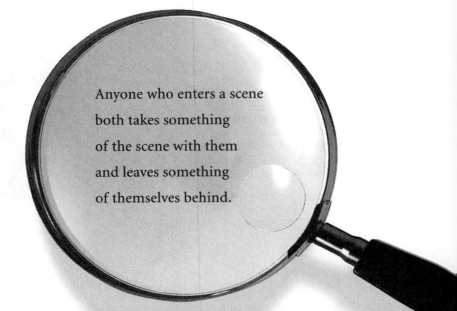

Anyone who enters a scene both takes something of the scene with them and leaves something of themselves behind.

For example, a person committing a crime might get dirt on his shoes and clothing at the crime scene, just as he would leave behind tiny traces of dust or fibres from his clothing and shoes. It was up to scientists to find the trace evidence and prove where it had come from.

Two years after Locard established his crime laboratory, he was asked to help with a murder investigation. A young woman had been found dead, and the most obvious suspect was her boyfriend. Unfortunately the boyfriend had an alibi. Some of his friends swore he was drinking with them at the time his girlfriend was murdered, and so he couldn't have done it.

Then Locard was called in. He examined the dead woman's body. He noticed marks around her neck that indicated she'd been strangled. Next he examined the boyfriend's hands and took scrapings from under his fingernails. Under the microscope Locard found flakes of skin that could have come from the dead woman.

He also found traces of her face powder. When the boyfriend was confronted with this evidence, he confessed.

Locard's *Principle of Exchange* is the reason why CSU (Crime Scene Unit) officers search for 'trace evidence': paint chips, fabric, dirt, blood, body fluids, footprints – almost anything you can think of. If they can match material found at the crime scene to a suspect, they have established a scientific link between the two. Of course, there may be perfectly innocent reasons for a person being at the crime scene. They might have been there before the crime was committed, or arrived afterwards. But even this information can help the police with their investigation.

6

MAGGOTS AND BLOODSTAINS

Sometimes bodies are not discovered for days or even weeks, and it can be difficult to establish exactly when the person died. This is when insects and maggots can help scientists determine the time of death, and possibly help solve the crime!

THAT'S OUR FRANKIE GRADUATING FROM THE POLICE ACADEMY.

YOU MUST BE SO PROUD

Within minutes of death, flies arrive at a decomposing body and start laying eggs. The eggs hatch into maggots that feed off the body and begin to grow, until the mature maggot forms a hard shell (a pupa). Inside the pupa, the maggot undergoes metamorphosis and changes into a fly, which will eventually emerge from the pupa and fly away (just like butterflies). Different species of fly take different lengths of time for each stage of growth and development.

Most maggots looks pretty much the same. Maggots collected from a crime scene are hatched inside a laboratory so that the adult fly can be identified.

Once entomologists (scientists who study insects) identify the species, they can calculate how long ago the flies arrived at the body, and when the person died!

BLOOD EVIDENCE

The presence of blood has always been of interest to crime detectives.

Even in ancient times, if a blood-spattered corpse was discovered, anybody caught nearby with bloodstains on their clothing was likely to be accused of murder! Innocent people were probably executed because they'd had a nosebleed or slaughtered a chicken for dinner.

It was not until 1901 that a German doctor developed a test to tell the difference between human and animal blood.

DO YOU KNOW WHAT BLOOD TYPE YOU ARE?

UM... RED?

This was unlucky for a French murderer the next year, who claimed the blood on his clothing was from skinning a rabbit. The new test proved him to be a liar. It was human blood, and he was sent to the guillotine.

Once scientists could tell if blood was human or not, the next step was to discover *whose* blood it was.

BLOOD GROUPS

Blood is a mixture of red and white blood cells suspended in a watery liquid called plasma. Certain chemicals carried by the red blood cells are called antigens. When different antigens come into contact with each other they cause red blood cells to clump together (which can make you terminally sick). It's the reason why blood transfusions must be from a compatible blood group.

At the beginning of the twentieth century an Austrian biologist identified three distinct types of antigen reaction. He called them group A (antigen A) group B (antigen B) and group O (no antigen).

Now forensic scientists could determine not only if the blood was human, but also identify the blood group. About 40 per cent of people are group A, about 40 per cent are group O, and 15 per cent group B. Only 5 per cent of people are group AB.

There were still problems when both the victim and the accused had the same blood group. Another antigen, the Rhesus factor, was discovered. People could either have it (Rh positive) or not (Rh negative). Since then other identifying chemicals have been isolated in human blood, including the most important of all, DNA.

DNA: THE GENETIC 'FINGERPRINT'

Human beings are composed of about a hundred million million cells.

Inside each cell is a nucleus, which contains very long thread-like structures, called chromosomes. Every human cell has 46 chromosomes – 23 are inherited from your mother, and 23 from your father.

Chromosomes are the building blocks of life; they decide what every single cell does. They determine if you are right- or left-handed, if you are blue- or brown-eyed. They determine the colour of your hair and the shape of your nose, how tall you will be, and if you're likely to get certain diseases.

In the first few decades of the twentieth century scientists discovered a special substance inside the cell's nucleus – they called it DNA (deoxyribose nucleic acid).

By the middle of the century scientists realised chromosomes were composed of DNA – and were in fact a 'genetic fingerprint'. No two people (apart

from identical twins) have the same set of chromosomes.

It still took many years to develop a scientific method to process and identify DNA. The first arrest and conviction on DNA evidence took place in England in 1987. Since then, DNA evidence has been used regularly by police and the courts.

BLOODSTAINS

Bloodstains at a crime scene (or on a suspect) can reveal other secrets. Adults have 6 to 8 litres of blood circulating inside their body. That's a lot of blood to leave at a crime scene. It's almost impossible to clean away all traces of blood, and even years later blood can be detected in cracks and crevices, or under floorboards and tiles. Today, scientists use sophisticated tests that can detect even the smallest trace of blood.

The pattern of bloodstains, or splatter, can provide forensic scientists and detectives with other clues.

When a drop of blood falls onto a horizontal surface, the stain will be circular. If the blood drops from a height (about two metres), the drop 'explodes' on contact and creates a star-shaped pattern.

Drops of blood from a moving source create an exclamation-mark pattern, and can reveal the direction of movement of the victim or the murder weapon.

Blood sprays and spurts can indicate the violence of the blows, and the injuries done to the victim. Pools of blood may indicate where the victim died, or if the body was shifted.

Police forces around the world have become very good at catching crooks. But sometimes there aren't any witnesses or physical evidence. How do you catch a crook then? How do you tell if someone's lying or telling the truth?

7

RIGHT OR LEFT?

THE LANGUAGE OF LYING

The Zulu people in Africa used a very cunning method to identify liars. Suspects were fed a spoonful of flour and then told to start talking. People who were telling the truth swallowed before speaking, while liars spat out dry flour. How did this happen? Did it work?

The Zulus were good observers of people's behaviour. When people are under stress (as when they are telling a lie) their bodies undergo physical changes.

Their heart beats faster, their blood pressure rises, their skin becomes sweaty, and their mouth becomes dry. A Zulu who was lying was unable to produce enough saliva to swallow!

Polygraph machines (lie detectors) work in much the same way – they measure changes in heart rate, blood pressure and sweating. But of course people can be under stress for many reasons, not just because they're guilty or lying. They might be tired and upset, hungry or thirsty. Being drunk or taking medication can affect the results. And skilled and practised liars feel no stress at all when telling lies, and so beat the polygraph. It is an unreliable method at best.

Police detectives will also watch a suspect's 'body language' while he is being questioned. Liars have to think fast as they make up their lies, and while they do so they tend to sit still and make fewer hand movements than non-liars. Generally they fidget, or touch their face and neck nervously while they lie.

Even which way the suspect glances while telling his story might help reveal the truth. People unconsciously glance to their right when they're remembering, and to the left when they're using the creative part of their brain and making stuff up!

None of these methods is foolproof. Practised liars can train themselves not to make obvious mistakes. It's claimed that the people who are best at detecting lies are not police detectives, but mothers!

TRIAL BY QUESTIONING

During the seventeenth century, people decided that instead of using magic and superstition to discover who was lying and who was telling the truth, they'd use science and logic. They believed careful questioning and the scientific investigation of evidence would uncover the truth. The best way to find out if someone was lying was to ask them questions, and then check their answers against the physical evidence, and other people's statements.

We still use this approach in our legal system today.

CRIMINAL BEHAVIOUR AND FBI PROFILING

In the mid-1970s several FBI detectives began to question convicted serial killers not only about their crimes, but also about their lives. The detectives were searching for ways to help identify and catch dangerous criminals.

The detectives discovered a link between behaviour and personality. What you do reveals a lot about who you are.

What could people learn about you by examining your bedroom when you're not there? Is it a mess, or so clean you could eat off the floor? Are there posters of sporting heroes or rock stars on the wall?

Is it full of computer games or sporting gear? Your behaviour (what you have and what you do) reflects your personality (messy or neat, athletic or studious).

From the evidence of your bedroom, we can probably predict where you'll be at lunchtime – whether it's in the library, or on the sports oval. Maybe you could predict who was the last member of your family to use the kitchen by examining the evidence left on the benches!

In a similar way, the FBI could make predictions about the personality of the offender by studying the crime scene. This is called 'psychological profiling'.

A typical offender profile might include information such as physical build, what sort of work the offender is likely to do, how old they are and if they own a car and what sort of vehicle it's likely to be!

Forensic psychologists will also carefully study the victim. By finding out his or her age, appearance, lifestyle, occupation, medical history and what he or she was doing just before the crime, they may discover clues about why the offender chose that particular victim.

WHERE DO CROOKS LIVE?

By studying the location of crimes, police detectives and forensic psychologists can also predict where an offender might live. This is called criminal geographic targeting (CGT).

All of us have mental maps of the place we live in. We feel most comfortable in areas that we know well – our homes, schools and workplaces. These are called our comfort zones. The size of our mental map will depend on several things, including whether we have to walk, or use public transport, or can drive a car.

Criminals have the same mental picture of their world. They like to do their crimes in an area they know well – they'll want to know the best escape routes, or places to hide. They'll have to work out if they're going to have to walk home afterwards, or catch a train or a bus. Have they got a car? Where will they leave it, and how quickly can they make their getaway?

They won't stay too close to home, though. If you're going to do a crime, you would be best to do it far enough away that you're not likely to run into people you know (like your mum or your next-door neighbour).

Like everyone else, criminals learn and gain confidence with experience. A criminal might try his first crime not too far away from where he lives. As he gains in confidence he will move further afield.

It's the reason police are very interested in the first crime in a series. It's likely to be close to where the offender lives or works or goes to school.

Detectives and psychologists can even predict how people behave when fleeing from a crime scene. Right-handed criminals will flee to their left and take the first left-hand turn they come to, while they'll dispose of any weapon or incriminating evidence to their right. Left-handed criminals will do the exact opposite!

People who are lost will also turn to their left or right depending on which hand they use. And men will walk downhill while women walk uphill. Trackers can use this information when they organise a search. A right-handed man will head off in a different direction to a left-handed woman.

PROFILING IN ACTION

A retired FBI detective was asked by an insurance company to review an insurance claim.

A woman reported that her house had been broken into and damaged by young vandals. There was obscene graffiti spray-painted on the walls, overturned furniture, and smashed ornaments and pictures. The police were satisfied with the original investigation, but the insurance company wasn't so sure . . .

The detective asked to see photos of the crime scene. Then he asked a few questions about the crime and the woman.

The insurance company told him she lived on her own. She was divorced and her daughter had recently left home to go to college. The woman had no financial problems, and the money from the claim would only cover the cost of repairing the damage. Fortunately, the vandals had not damaged a very valuable ornament on the mantelpiece, or a treasured photograph of her daughter.

The detective was immediately suspicious.

He knew from experience that vandals aren't selective about what they damaged. They usually smash everything. It was too much of a coincidence that the only picture that wasn't damaged was the one of the woman's daughter. Similarly, why had only the valuable ornament survived, while all the others were smashed? Finally, the graffiti was sprayed at the same height on the walls, which didn't fit if there were several vandals, and the words used sounded more like a middle-aged woman than a young offender . . .

The detective suggested the insurance company should confront the woman. She broke down and confessed she'd vandalised her own house.

She was lonely, and she hoped the insurance money would pay for her to redecorate. She admitted she couldn't bring herself to destroy the picture of her daughter, or the valuable ornament.

The insurance company didn't pay the claim, and the woman was charged with insurance fraud.

8

CAUGHT IN COURT

Today we use evidence in a court of law to prove a person's guilt. Police collect physical evidence and witnesses' statements. Lawyers present this material in a court to a judge (and/or a jury), who will listen to the evidence and decide if the accused person is guilty or innocent.

Most English-speaking countries (including Australia and the USA) use a *common law* legal system. It is based on the common rules and customs used over many centuries in England. The accused person is presumed to be innocent. It is the prosecution's responsibility to prove them guilty beyond reasonable doubt.

Many European countries, as well as Latin America and parts of Africa and Asia, use a *civil law* justice system. It is based on the laws of Ancient Rome. The accused person is presumed to be guilty. It is the accused person's responsibility to prove their own innocence.

KIDS AND THE LAW

Most countries (but not all) have special laws and courts for children.

Children under the age of eight (ten in some places) cannot be charged with a criminal offence. They are considered to be too young to tell the difference between right and wrong, or understand the consequences of their actions. Little kids playing with matches might not understand that they can burn down the house!

Between the ages of eight and fourteen, children are expected to take some responsibility for their actions. Not only must the prosecution prove that the child is guilty of a crime, but also that they are old enough to understand that what they did was wrong.

Children older than fourteen are presumed to have the same understanding of right and wrong as adults.

Children's courts are different from ordinary courts. The welfare of the child, rather than punishment, is the court's first priority.

KIDS AND THE POLICE

If the police want to speak to you, remember to be calm and polite.

> NO
> SKATING
> SKATEBOARDING
> OR
> BICYCLING
> BEYOND THIS POINT
> BY POLICE ORDER

If the police suspect you of breaking (or being about to break) a law, or if they think you have information about a serious crime, they have the right to ask for your name and address.

If you are driving a vehicle or riding a pushbike, travelling on public transport, or in a place selling alcohol, they also have the right to ask for your name and address.

It is an offence to refuse, or to give a false name and address. You can be arrested if you do.

If you're in a public place, the police have the right to search you if they think you're carrying drugs, stolen goods or weapons. They can ask you to turn out your pockets and take off your jacket. They can also search anything you're carrying, or the vehicle you're travelling in. If you're at school, the police can only search you if the principal agrees.

It is against the law to carry weapons.

It is against the law to carry any sort of knives – flick knives, daggers, butterfly knives or knuckle knives. It is against the law to carry weapons like

WOULD SOMEONE GET
THE ACCUSED SOME
PHONE-BOOKS

nunchakus, capsicum spray, slingshots, throwstars or knuckledusters.

Some weapons, like chef's knives, can be carried lawfully if they're used for work or sport. You will have to prove this.

Self-defence is not a lawful excuse for carrying weapons. Carrying weapons is against the law and you can be arrested for it.

If you are arrested or taken into custody, the police have a right to question you if they believe a delay might allow another suspect to escape, or if someone is in danger.

If you are under seventeen, the police may not formally question you until your parents or guardians are there. If your parents aren't available (or you don't want them to be there) another independent person must be with you to make sure you understand your rights and what is going on. An independent person does not give legal advice.

You have the right to speak to a lawyer before you talk to the police. A lawyer will give you legal advice.

9

JUSTICE GONE WRONG

Even with all our modern policing and scientific detection methods, innocent people are still convicted and sent to jail. As well as proving guilt, DNA evidence can sometimes prove people's innocence.

In 1984 a man named Kirk Bloodsword was found guilty of the rape and murder of a nine-year-old girl in Washington, USA. It was a terrible crime and he was sentenced to death. He spent eight years in prison, including two years on 'Death Row' waiting to be executed. Kirk Bloodsword continued to protest his innocence, though no one believed him.

Then in 1992, after DNA testing had been discovered, the evidence in his case was re-examined. Body fluids found at the scene of the crime did not match Kirk Bloodsword's DNA. The next year he became the first person to be released from jail because DNA testing had proved his innocence.

Since then hundreds of prisoners waiting on Death Row in the USA have been released because of DNA testing. In Florida alone, twenty-four men have been declared innocent. In 2002 the Governor of Illinois,

George Ryan, banned all executions because no one could be sure that the men waiting to be executed were really guilty!

But science doesn't always get it right.

A CRY IN THE WILDERNESS

On the night of 17 August 1980 the Chamberlain family were preparing dinner at a campsite near the base of Ayers Rock (Uluru). The children were tired after a long day of sightseeing. Their mother, Lindy, put the youngest boy to bed in the tent before she put the new baby down to sleep in her bassinette next to him.

Lindy returned to the campsite with a tin of baked beans for supper. A few minutes later someone said they thought they heard a baby crying. Lindy went to investigate. As she approached the tent she saw an animal emerge with something in its mouth, and quickly slink off into the darkness. Lindy hurried into the tent and checked the bassinette. The baby, Azaria, was gone. She rushed back to the campsite.

'A dingo's got my baby!' she screamed.

Immediately everyone began to search the area. They found nothing but a few drops of blood inside the tent, and animal tracks leading off into the darkness. There was no sign of Azaria.

A week later, torn and bloody baby clothes were found near a dingo's cave, and Mrs Chamberlain identified then as the ones the baby was wearing. Only one piece of clothing was missing – a knitted matinee jacket. It didn't seem very important at the time. The Chamberlains returned home after their nightmare holiday – but their real nightmare was just about to begin.

The rumours started. People couldn't believe dingoes were dangerous, and if it wasn't a dingo that killed the baby it must have been the Chamberlains. The Chamberlains' religious beliefs came under suspicion. People said that the baby's name, Azaria, actually meant 'sacrifice in the wilderness' and that Lindy dressed Azaria in black clothes and had a tiny coffin in their house.

The case was re-opened and forensic scientists examined the Chamberlains' car and camping gear. The police were convinced Lindy was guilty of murder. Nearly two years after Azaria disappeared, Lindy was charged and sent for trial.

The forensic scientists testified that baby's blood had been found in the car – a pool of blood under the seat, and a fine spray under the dashboard. One scientist testified that the tears in the baby's clothes were not made by dingoes, but by scissors. One expert even claimed to find a bloody human handprint on the baby's jumpsuit!

'If a dingo took the baby, why wasn't there any dingo saliva on the baby's clothes?' the prosecution asked Lindy.

When Lindy protested that Azaria had been wearing a matinee jacket over the baby clothes, she was called a liar. Lindy and Michael Chamberlain were found guilty of murder, and she was sent to jail.

Nearly five years after Lindy Chamberlain was sent to jail, a British tourist fell to his death from Ayers Rock. His body was found eight days later not far from a dingo's lair. Police were searching the area when a ranger noticed something buried in the sand. He pulled it out. It was a tiny knitted baby's jacket.

Lindy Chamberlain was released from jail a few days later.

The forensic tests and scientific evidence were re-examined. The 'blood' in the Chamberlains' car proved to be a spilt milkshake. The spray pattern under the dashboard was not baby's blood, but insulation put there during manufacture! The bloody 'handprint' didn't exist. All the things people had said proved to be just cruel rumours. There were no black baby clothes. Azaria actually meant 'beloved of God'. Other dingo attacks were reported. Lindy hadn't lied about the matinee jacket, or anything else that happened that

terrible night at Ayers Rock when Azaria was taken and killed by a dingo.

So why were the Chamberlains convicted of murder?

It was a bit like a medieval witch trial. The Chamberlains were in a 'no win' situation. Once people (and the police) became convinced that the Chamberlains were guilty, evidence was used to fit that belief. It didn't matter what the Chamberlains said; it didn't even matter that they were telling the truth. They were believed to be guilty – so they must be lying.

10

DOES CRIME EVER PAY?

The big problem for criminals is that once they've started to lie, steal and cheat to get what they want, they find out it's very difficult to stop. They have to change their behaviour, and most people find that a very hard thing to do. And if criminals keep breaking the law, sooner or later they're going to get caught.

But what about people who get away with crimes? Does crime pay for them?

DB COOPER –
THE PERFECT CRIME?

On 24 November 1971, in the USA, a middle-aged man walked up to the Northwest Airlines ticket counter at Portland International Airport.

He identified himself as Dan Cooper, took off his sunglasses and bought a one-way ticket on a flight to Seattle. He paid for the ticket in cash.

He was smartly dressed in a dark suit, tie and white shirt, and carried a briefcase and overcoat over one arm. He was just another businessman in the crowded airport. No one gave him a second glance.

He boarded the plane just after four o'clock in the afternoon.

The plane was less than a quarter full, and 'Dan Cooper' sat in row 18 by himself.

I'D LIKE A TICKET TO SEATTLE

ONE-WAY?

HALF-WAY ACTUALLY.

TICK TICK TICK

He calmly handed the stewardess a note, which she slipped into her pocket while she got the other passengers ready for take-off.

The stewardess didn't read the note until the plane was in the air. In the note Dan Cooper demanded $200 000 in unmarked bills, plus four parachutes. He warned against any 'funny stuff', as he was carrying a bomb. She immediately alerted the flight crew, who contacted the airport and asked for instructions.

The stewardess was sent back to talk to Dan Cooper to see if he really had a bomb. He briefly opened his suitcase and showed her 'some red cylinders and wires'. Everyone took the threat seriously.

The plane circled above Seattle airport until the money and parachutes were ready. The FBI agents just had time to run the 10 000 $20 bills through a new high-speed photocopier. The plane landed and the passengers were allowed to leave, before the money and parachutes were handed over.

Dan Cooper then demanded that the plane be flown to Mexico. He insisted that the pilot fly the jet below 10 000 feet, with the landing gear down and the wing flaps set at 15 degrees. This would slow the plane down and make it possible to use a parachute.

A few minutes after take-off, Dan Cooper asked the stewardess to show him how to open the rear door of the plane. Then he told her to return to the front of the plane and remain with the rest of the crew. She glanced back briefly as she left, in time to see the hijacker tying something around his waist, which she assumed was the bag of money.

Not long afterwards the pilot noticed a red warning light. The rear door of the plane was open. If they had been flying at their normal altitude, the plane would have instantly exploded. The pilot hit the intercom.

'Is everything OK back there? Is there anything we can do for you?' the pilot asked.

'No,' came the shouted reply.

A few minutes later the pilot felt 'pressure bumps', which the FBI later assumed was Dan Cooper leaving the aircraft.

Dan Cooper jumped into the pitch-black night wearing only a suit and overcoat, with a ten-kilo bag of money tied around his waist. His shoes would have been blown off his feet the instant he left the plane. If his parachute failed, he would have hit the ground fifteen seconds later. If it opened, he would have landed in a heavily treed wilderness crisscrossed with frozen rivers in sub-zero temperatures.

The plane was searched when it landed. The only thing left behind by Dan Cooper was his tie and tie-pin.

A storm over the next two days hampered the search, but more than 300 men combed the snow-filled forest for over a month. Not a trace of Dan Cooper or the money was found.

Nearly nine years later, a boy found $5800 in badly decomposed $20 bills in a sandy riverbank. The notes were identified as part of the missing money, and the boy received a reward. After that, despite a huge investigation, the trail went cold.

After the Dan Cooper hijack, airports introduced new security regulations. They set up metal detectors and searched passengers' hand luggage. Commercial aircraft were modified so doors could not be opened in-flight.

WHAT HAPPENED TO DAN COOPER?

The case of D.B. Cooper remains open. The name
he gave at the airport was false, and he was never
identified. His fingerprints weren't on file. There was
no missing person report that matched his description.
No one knows who he was.

FBI agents assume he is dead; either 'splattered'
when his parachute failed, or frozen to death in the
wilderness.

Other people speculate that he survived and is living in Florida or Canada or Argentina.

A list of the serial numbers of the $20 bills is still in circulation.

A PRICE TO PAY

If D. B. Cooper were still alive he would be an old man who has spent the last thirty-odd years of his life looking over his shoulder, knowing he could be arrested at any moment. Unable to spend the money without leaving a trail, he faces very serious criminal charges and a lengthy prison sentence if he's ever caught, even today.

HOW TO RUIN YOUR LIFE

Four hundred years ago an English playwright, William Shakespeare, wrote about how crime changed people's lives. His play *Macbeth* is a tragic story of ambition, betrayal and murder.

Macbeth was a loyal nobleman much loved by his king, Duncan. But Macbeth was ambitious and believed it was his fate to be king. Lady Macbeth was even more ambitious than her husband was, and she urged him on, convincing him that the quickest way to get what they wanted was to kill the king. When Duncan came to stay at their castle, they had the opportunity to put their plan into action. Macbeth stabbed the king to death while he was asleep, and afterwards Lady Macbeth smeared the sleeping servants with blood and 'framed' them for the murder.

Although some people were suspicious, Macbeth was proclaimed king. But Lady Macbeth began to have nightmares and she wandered the castle at night trying to wash the blood off her hands. Finally, driven mad by guilt, she died. As for Macbeth, he discovered that no one trusted him any more. Worse, in order to keep his crown, he had to kill anyone who stood in his way. In the end, Macbeth met his own tragic death and was killed.

The problem was that Macbeth and Lady Macbeth thought they'd still be the same people after they'd murdered the king. They believed they'd be king and queen and everyone would love them. They'd get what they wanted and nothing would change. Shakespeare realised that people have to live with the consequences of their actions. Doing crimes changes how other people think about us – they may no longer trust us, or believe what we say. But worst of all, doing crimes changes *us*. We don't become really nice people who just happen to steal and cheat; we become thieves and liars. One way or another, crime doesn't pay.

BEVERLEY MacDONALD is a law-abiding citizen. She writes stories about the weird stuff in science and history. Her non-fiction books for children include *Big Bangs* and *Written in Blood*, both illustrated by the very weird Andrew Weldon.

ANDREW WELDON is not a criminal. You can't prove it. The case was dropped due to lack of evidence, OK? Won't you people leave him alone? Also, he draws cartoons.

CRIME DICTIONARY

Here are some useful words and phrases to do with detecting, crime and police. If you don't know their meaning after reading this book, look them up in a dictionary.

arson
at knifepoint, at gunpoint
body language
civil law system
common law system
convict (also conviction)
Death Row
deductive reasoning
DNA

forensic
highwayman
latent fingerprints
morgue
nunchakus
ordeal (also trial by ordeal)
phrenology
private investigator (or PI)
prosecution
psychological profiling
scaffold
taken into custody
throwstars
transportation
witness (also bearing witness,
   bearing false witness)

FURTHER INVESTIGATION

Policemen and women are trained at special police schools. People who want to be detectives must first work as police officers before they are selected for detective training. If you'd like to find out more about police and detectives you can visit you local police force's website for information about what they do, and how you can apply for a career in the police force. Your local police force may have a 'Police in Schools' program, and will send an officer to talk to your school.

Forensic scientists must complete a science degree at university before undertaking special training. They are generally employed by the Coroner's Court, which investigates what happened when a person dies unexpectedly or because of an accident. Your state's Coroner's Court website will provide more information about what they do, and what subjects you must study at school if you are interested in a career in forensic science. It may also be possible to organise a school visit to the court, and work experience for high-school students.

Forensic pathologists must first be trained as doctors before they undertake further study. Visit your local Institute of Forensic Medicine's website for further information.

Court proceedings are open to the public, and it may be possible to organise a tour of your local Magistrate's Court to see how it operates.

INDEX